I0571632

The Ultimate Lifeguard

AMYANN BAUMAN

CONTENTS

THE ULTIMATE LIFEGUARD

INTRODUCTION

I first went through lifeguard training when I was eighteen years old. I was working as a missionary with an organization called Teen Missions International. Every summer Teen Missions had, and still has, a summer program for teenagers and preteens. The program starts with training at a camp called The Lord's Boot Camp and then each group goes to the country or state their mission is located.

While training at The Lord's Boot Camp, the kids are allowed to swim and wash clothes at the lake during free time, so they named that lake Bathtub Lake. The team with the cleanest tent site and eating area gets to swim in the pool!

I life guarded at the pool, Bathtub Lake and other places around the property, but I liked the pool the most because I could see everything that was in the water. All the lifeguards at boot camp wanted to lifeguard at the pool. All the lifeguards at boot camp were qualified for the pool, but only the people who swam the extra laps could guard the lakes and water obstacle course. I remember a couple of people during training who wouldn't or couldn't do the extra laps, so they only guarded the pool.

In training, lifeguards learn how to keep the people they are responsible for safe. They are willing to go through hours of training and inconvenience to keep people from drowning or getting hurt.

In this world there are many things that can harm us. There are times when we feel like we are floating on an inflatable tube down Lazy River, other times it feels like we are drowning in the middle of the ocean with no hope of rescue. God sees where each of us are. He has done the extra laps and is wanting to keep us from dangerous waters. He is the only One willing and qualified to lifeguard us spiritually and get us to the final shore.

God knows what waters are best for each of us and what rules are important to follow. He is willing to jump in and be there for us when we cry for help. He can and will provide safety during the storms we face as we fully trust Him and look to Him in those storms.

Throughout this book I will refer to Jesus as the Lifeguard (with a capital L). I will be going through each step a lifeguard must take in order to rescue a drowning victim, then tell you how it correlates with what Jesus has done and is doing as our Ultimate Lifeguard. At the end of each chapter there will be a section called *Dive Deeper*. This section is a study guide that can be used for just one person or a study group. All scripture verses are English Standard Version, unless told otherwise.

Obviously, you do not have to look up the scripture verses. But, in order for you to get more out of this book, I would highly recommend you read them. The more effort we put in, the more we will get out.

~ 1 ~

TRAINING

I did not choose to be a lifeguard, I was asked. While I was in Bible school I was approached by the school's coordinator. She was getting volunteers to go through training in order to lifeguard at boot camp.

For those of you who have not read my previous book, The Care Giver, I used to be a missionary with Teen Missions International. They do short term mission trips for young people. The first two weeks of their trip is training for their mission at the Lord's Boot Camp. Long story short, I went to Teen Missions a few times as a teenager, then became a leader and student at their Bible school.

The school's coordinator knew I was responsible, for the most part. One thing she did not know, is that I could not swim. Instead of letting her know I couldn't swim, I decided to learn so I could become a lifeguard.

Comfort Zone

Before I became a lifeguard I could not swim well. Anytime I would get in a pool I would stay in the shallow area or hold on to the sides. I never would have thought that I would be the one looking out for the safety of others in water.

First thing I had to do in order to become a licensed lifeguard is become a stronger swimmer. The side of the pool was my comfort zone. I had to leave my comfort zone in order for this to work. As we went through training I had to be willing to get away from the pool's side and work on the different strokes I was expected to be able to do. I had to be able to swim from one side of the pool to the other... with a brick.

As I said, I was in Bible school. I believe in Jesus as Christ and claim Him as my Heavenly Father and Savior. In this book I will be connecting Him as The Ultimate Lifeguard. There are many similarities and differences. Let's get started, shall we?

What's the Difference?
Body & Soul

Your typical lifeguard looks out for the physical safety of people while they swim. Jesus looks out for our eternal souls.

Solomon in Proverbs 4:23 talks about guarding our hearts.

"Keep your heart with all vigilance,
for from it flow the springs of life."

Many people have heard the story of Solomon's father, David; how he was a brave young man who killed a giant named Goliath, then later became king over the people of Israel. One part you may not have known is that he was anointed to be king over Israel before knocking down the giant.

David had been anointed by God through a priest named Samuel. Samuel was told by God to anoint someone to be king. You see, the current king, Saul was not being obedient and was allowing his position to get to his head instead of seeking God's guidance.

In 1 Samuel 16, God told Samuel (the priest) to go visit a man named Jesse and anoint one of his kids. Jesse had eight sons. One by one, Jesse had his seven oldest boys strut their stuff in front of Samuel. One by one God told Samuel no, he wasn't the one.

In verse 7 God told Samuel, "The Lord sees not as man sees: man looks on the outward appearance, but the Lord looks on the heart."

David's father did not think David was king material. When Samuel saw David, he didn't either. God was not looking at the package He had made, He was looking at the goods on the inside.

So as a regular lifeguard, I am trying to keep people alive and safe. God sees and guards our hearts and minds and is trying to renew the way we think and live (Romans 12:1-2)(Philippians 4:7).

Same Thing
For Your Safety

So we have our differences, but we have something very much in common. We both are looking out for the people in our watch. When you have a good lifeguard, you can rest easy, knowing you and your loved ones are safe under their protective watch. You can trust that they know what they are doing, because of their care and training. You can obey their rules, knowing they are there for your safety.

One thing that makes Jesus the best guard is that He is never caught off guard. He can see every person, no one is overlooked. He is not like Santa though, He is not watching you to see if you are naughty or nice, He is watching to keep you safe. He does the work, not you. He is also fit and very much non-fictional.

Lifeguard training can be hard on the body. You have to be at least relatively in shape in order to swim the distance and pull someone to the shore. Jesus is more than fit to pull us out of the puddles we've gotten ourselves into.

Qualification

In this chapter, I tell about some of what it takes to make someone a qualified lifeguard and what it took for Jesus to be THE qualified Lifeguard. In other chapters, I will be talking about some of that training and rescue and how it relates perfectly to Jesus.

Jesus came to earth to rescue us from our sins and the consequences of them. He was fully qualified. He is the most undiscriminating lifeguard you will ever meet. Romans 5 talks about how it would be hard to die for a good person, but Jesus died for us while we were against Him. Then it goes on to say in verses 9 and 10,
“Since, therefore, we have now been justified by his blood,
much more shall we be saved by him from the wrath of God.
For if while we were enemies we were reconciled to God
by the death of his Son, much more,
now that we are reconciled,
shall we be saved by his life.”

He went way beyond what other lifeguards would, He gave His life for the swimmers who were not obeying His rules. He made those rules to keep us safe and we were going against them. We were not just going against His rules, we were going against Him. And He died for us anyway!

As a lifeguard, I cared about the safety of the swimmers in my pool or lake, but honestly I'm not sure if I would be willing to die for them. Especially the disobedient ones.

In John 17, Jesus told the Father that He was guarding the people as priest. It was the priest's job to not only anoint rulers, but to pray for the people and intercede for them. And that is what Jesus does for us. In verse 19 Jesus said that He consecrated Himself so that we could be sanctified in truth. In other words, Jesus came to earth and to the cross so we could be made holy.

In lifeguard talk: Jesus was the only qualified Lifeguard for our souls. He went through “training” for us so He could be our eternal Lifeguard. I'll let you know what that fully means as we go.

Yes, there is a huge difference between me as an imperfect human lifeguard and Christ as our eternal Savior. But, I hope and pray you understand the connection. As a "swimmer" under God's watch, I am redeemed. Because Christ died and rose for me and I have placed my faith and trust in Him; He guards my heart, renews my mind, and has assured me spiritual life even after my physical body dies.

What It Takes

It takes hours of training to be a lifeguard. I sat through several hours of lectures to know things like how to pop a shoulder back in place, which came in handy later on. We all appreciated the indoor training, because it was mostly in an air conditioned room, but some of us got pretty queasy with some of the pictures that were shown! Somethings you had to know from the instruction book before you could practice in the water.

We practiced CPR and first aid. Some things we practiced using dummies. Some things we practiced on each other. There were a few things we just had to know and pray we never had to experience.

In order to qualify and get a lifeguard license, I had to pass tests on paper, tests on the shore, and tests in the water. I had to be "book smart" and physically able to rescue someone.

The Bible says "the Word became flesh." (John 1:14) This is talking about Jesus. He not only knew the book, He was the Book. He was who all the Messianic prophecies were about. Any time it speaks about what love is, they are speaking about Him.

Jesus was "Book smart." He knew the manual. Jesus knew what was commanded and how to live. He totally passed the written test.

He didn't just know, He did. He became a man and put into practice what was said. He never said, "Do as I say, not as I do." He lived the perfect example. He was/is the perfect Lifeguard. He not only passed the written test, but the shore and water tests too.

Later, we will talk about how Jesus controls the water and is preparing the shore for us. As we live, we have a choice to make; we can float through this life, hoping we make it to shore or we can ask for the Lifeguard to show us how we can live a life above the water and know what type of shore awaits us.

Dive Deeper

A lifeguard looks at the body. The Lifeguard looks at the soul. It is so easy to get caught up in the temporary things of this world. If you are a child of The King, you have nothing to fear. Your Lifeguard is looking out for you. Not everything on the earth will be easy, but all those temporary struggles are just that: temporary.

You are a temporary swimmer, but a permanent prince/princess. As you swim through life, I want to encourage you by letting you know that with The Lifeguard you might not swim forever, but if you have Jesus as your Lifeguard, you can live forever with Him.

Memory Verse:

"And the peace of God, which surpasses all understanding, will guard your hearts and your minds in Christ Jesus."
Philippians 4:7

If you haven't already, you should read John 17. If you are in a study group, talk about it.

King Saul allowed his position to get to his head and forgot who gave him that position. Have you ever been in a situation where you forgot about who got you where you are?

Romans 12:2 says, "Do not be conformed to this world, but be transformed by the renewal of your mind, that by testing you may discern what is the will of God, what is good and acceptable and perfect."

God sees your heart and mind. He made them and the wrapping that covers them. Has God transformed you in any way? Testify how God has started a good work in you and pray for each other in areas He still needs to renew.

Packages can be so misleading. I have been so surprised and disappointed at times when I have opened something and it turned out totally different than what it shows on the case. In what way are your insides and outsides different?

Have you ever been misunderstood? I know I have. One thing I love about God is that He never misunderstands me. He sees my heart and mind and never misinterprets what I say. Does that encourage or frighten you?

Jesus is not watching you in order to call you out on all your flaws. He sometimes will see a flaw and show you how to swim better. As we read the Bible and start understanding it, we can understand God better. Is there anything about God that you may have misunderstood?

When a person is going through training, there is always an end goal. We will be going through the end goal later in this study, but for now, know that He did not train for a paycheck. He did not go through pain to be popular. He loves you and went through His "training" out of love for you. Please do not misunderstand His motives, He didn't get "licensed" to avoid liability, He did it because He is our only hope.

~ 2 ~

DANGER!

In the last chapter we went over training and qualifications of being a lifeguard. In this chapter we are going to look at how a lifeguard can usually see danger before the swimmer can. A lifeguard can see danger and potential danger because of their training and position.

In training we learn as a lifeguard we are to do what we can to prevent accidents from occurring, but when the danger comes we blow that whistle, get the other swimmers to safety, and help the person who is in danger. As the Ultimate Lifeguard, God does things a bit differently than we do and differently than we sometimes think He should. Every situation demands a different response.

Potential Accidents

When I was on duty I could see potential accidents happening and let the person about to cause the accident to correct their actions. Most of the time people would follow instructions and things went "swimmingly." Every now and then a person would ignore me and there were different results.

When it was a serious affiance, I would call them out of the pool before something serious could happen. Sometimes I would have someone get out of the pool for their safety, sometimes it was for the safety of someone else.

There were a couple of times someone would scrape their knee or have a minor injury. Occasionally, a rebellious person had no immediate consequence and they moved on with their life.

No Guessing

Our Ultimate Lifeguard does not guess what will happen, He knows. When I stop to think about this, it's crazy that we sometimes ignore Him. He knows when we should or should not take action. He has already given some instructions in stone for everyone and yet, we ignore the Lifeguard. He knows we can enjoy our time in and out of the water so much more when we follow the rules. Then we can live without regrets or as many hurts.

There are times when the offender does not see the results of their actions right away. I don't always understand why God doesn't teach some people a lesson right away, but does others. I do not always comprehend why He teaches some people one way and others another. But, one thing I do know is, every person is different and has different needs and ways of learning. God knows each person's learning style and needs. His goal is not to fulfill our every whim. He loves us and wants us to have the best life and make us into the best form of us we can be. He also knows what it will take for us to get there.

Get Out!

I remember one boy who kept doing the dead man float. (For those of you who do not know what that is, it is when someone holds their breath and floats face down in the water.) I told this kid to not do it anymore, because I had no way of telling when he is faking and when he is in distress. He did it again, so I told him he had to get out of the pool for the rest of his free time.

I hope this isn't too much information, but one day while I was life-guarding at a lake I was told that someone had pooped in the water. It did not take much investigating to find that they were telling me the truth! I got everyone out of that part of the lake. Some of the swimmers were upset and did not know why they were forced to stop swimming. It wasn't the type of announcement I could have given with a strait face and I didn't find it a necessary one. Some of the people understood and others didn't. As the kids were getting out of the water, I saw the snout of an alligator. Everyone got out safely and most people did not know about the gator or the deposit that had been made. Sometimes God uses stinky things in life to guide us to safer waters.

There were times I would blow my whistle for everyone to get out of the pool so I could help one who was in danger. There were a couple of times I asked someone to get out for reasons unknown to the other swimmers. I always had a reason and it was always for the safety of the people in my care.

I Don't Understand

I do not know why God calls some people out of this earth when He does, but I know He is working for our good and knows what He is doing.

King Hezekiah, when he got over being sick said, "Behold, it was for my welfare that I had great bitterness; but in love you have delivered my life from the pit of destruction, for you have cast all my sins behind your back." (Isaiah 38:17)

There have been so many times I went through tough situations that I did not understand while I was going through them, but afterwards saw it was good for my spirit to go through that rough patch. In love God lets us go through things and with love delivers us from the pit of destruction. I will go into details in later chapters how we have to trust Him in order for Him to rescue us. But for now, just know that God doesn't want anyone to perish and we will not always understand why He does or doesn't do things.

Know It All

When I was a lifeguard I would rather lifeguard for the pool than the lakes any day. The main reason was because I could see everything in the water at the pool. At the lakes I did not see everything under the surface and did not want to be unpleasantly surprised by any unseen creature.

When a lifeguard starts their shift, they choose a spot where they can see all the swimmers. If there is more than one lifeguard, they cover each others' blind spots to insure everyone's safety.

One thing God and I have in common is we are looking out for others in the water. Something we do not have in common is God sees everyone and everything, He has no blind spots. He sees what is under the dirty waters we sometimes swim in. He is never surprised by them or caught off guard. Later, I will talk about how He was willing to get in those dirty waters to save us.

Listen to the Whistle

A lifeguard can blow the whistle to get swimmers out of the water. We do not always know why the lifeguard is asking someone to get out, but there is always a reason. I have gotten people out for various reasons: someone peed in the pool, there's an alligator, there's lightning, someone needs attention and I need to get swimmers to safety before giving that attention. Whether you understand the reason or not, do you really want to go against The Lifeguard who sees better than you and knows what is coming when you don't? Every person has to make their own choices on this, but I want to listen and obey my Lifeguard.

When a lifeguard blows their whistle it is not always to get people out of the pool. When I was a lifeguard I would instruct each group what to do if I blew my whistle. When I blew it once, the swimmers needed to stop what they were doing, look at me and wait for instructions. I let them know before they got in what I expected and what to expect from me.

Whistle Blow

Jesus has already seen the danger of your life without His help. He has done the training and is wanting you to stop what you are doing and look at Him. The Bible tells us about the warnings He has given. Now it is up to the swimmers to take heed to His instructions.

Whether we understand them yet or not, He has told us what He expects and what to expect from Him. There is no need for misunderstandings, God has told us what He has done, why He has done it and what we need to do.

I will be talking about these things throughout the book, but for now, has God been "blowing His whistle" at you? If He is trying to get your attention, please don't ignore Him. He is not trying to get your attention just to get you to stop swimming and take away your fun so He can have a snack break. He might want to show you a better way to swim, warn you of danger, or get you to help another swimmer.

A good lifeguard does their best to prevent dangerous situations. That is why you usually hear lifeguards say things like, "Walk please!" It is up to us to obey the Lifeguard or go against Him. Just know, there are always consequences to the choices we make. Let's obey our Lifeguard instead of getting mad at Him for things we don't understand or for Him doing His job.

It is easier to see what is going on around a swimmer when watching from outside the water. God is everywhere, He sees what you are going through from your perspective, but also from the side and above. He understands when you want to keep swimming and keep having fun, but He is working to keep you safe, and sometimes that means fun takes a backseat.

Chapter 3 Preview

My favorite place to lifeguard was at the pool because I could see through the water and there was nothing swimming in the water other than people (and one time there was a snake).

The water obstacle course at boot camp was my least favorite place to guard because there was a tunnel that I had to check for debris...and alligators! Thankfully, I never found one, but it was a bit scary knowing it was a possibility!

I did not like going in the water. I did not have to go in the water. But, in order to assure the safety of my swimmers, I went in. In the next chapter I am going to cover a lifeguard's willingness to get in. But for now, I want to leave you with this thought:

Since God can see all and knows what is going on on the surface and in the dirtiest water, let's listen to the warnings He gives.

Dive Deeper

Memory Verse:
James 1:22
"But be doers of the word,
and not hearers only,
deceiving yourselves."

I would like for you to read James 1:19-27. In lifeguard speech it would look something like this:

*Fellow swimmers, please be quick to listen to the Lifeguard,
because He will save your life.
Pay attention to how He wants you to swim
because it is the only way to stay safe
and be able to truly enjoy yourself
and allow others to enjoy themselves.
Don't just hear His instructions, obey Him.
Anyone who thinks themselves a good swimmer
and ignores the Lifeguard is a moron.
They can be the best swimmer in the world,
but swimming well doesn't do you any good
when you are swimming with a shark,
whether he sees the shark or not.
The best way to swim is listen carefully to the Lifeguard
and follow the instructions given verbally and on the sign,
be considerate of other swimmers,
and don't do things that could damage the pool or it's reviews.*

Is there anything you caught in the scripture or my lifeguard interpretation of it that stood out to you?

Have there been moments you did not understand why God called someone out of the water or felt like God was trying to get your attention?

There have been moments in my life that I did not understand what God wanted me to do. Sometimes I know what He wants me to do, but I don't understand why. When I do not fully understand something, I have a hard time taking action. I don't like messing up and I don't like getting hurt. But, God has already said no one is perfect except Him (Romans 3:10-12), that means I will mess up. Because we all mess up, I will get hurt.

If you would step back into James 1 with me, you'll see in 1:2-12 that we will face difficult things, but when we do we need to ask our Lifeguard for help. We might not get everything we ask for, but He will watch out for us and provide what we need.

~ 3 ~

JUMP IN

I told you that lifeguards try to prevent dangers, but there are times when dangers come. When a lifeguard sees danger and the person is unable to get out of that danger on their own, the lifeguard jumps in. The lifeguard puts their life on the line for the swimmer and does what it takes to rescue them.

A lifeguard always needs to look out for their own safety while rescuing someone. One way a lifeguard protects him/herself is by going behind the person who's drowning so they can get to the person without getting pulled under the water.

Once the guard is behind the person, they put the rescue tube in between themselves and the swimmer, where it is positioned in front of the lifeguard and behind the swimmer. This position helps the lifeguard have more control and the tube can better support both people's weight.

Having the tube between the two people helps keep them both safe. Remember, a lifeguard is trying to stay safe while rescuing the person. This position helps them stay in control, not because they want to be a control-freak, but because this will make it easier for them to maneuver the person to safety. We will talk more about this part of the rescue in the next couple of chapters, so let's put a pin in this for now.

Sacrificial Rescue

Jesus didn't want to die, but His main objective was to rescue us from our sin. He was unlike the typical lifeguard, because He willingly died to rescue His swimmers, knowing this was the only way for you and me to be spiritually rescued. He did not put a tube between us and Himself. After diving into the water and sacrificing Himself, He was able to pull us on top of the water by faith in Him.

"For by grace you have been saved through faith.
And this is not your own doing;
it is the gift of God,"
Ephesians 2:8

The main concern of a lifeguard is for the people in the water to stay alive. We also do not want anyone to get hurt.

God is not willing that any should perish. (2 Peter 3:9) Jesus came not just to give us a physical life, but a real life that will last forever and is better than we could ever dream. (John 10:10)

In order for us to have this life overflowing with goodness, Jesus had to come to this earth, live a sinless life, die, and be risen from the dead. He did all of that! And He did it in order for us to truly live, by giving us the chance to follow Him.

Actions Louder than Words

God didn't just watch and blow a whistle, He got into the water for us. He didn't just send a love note, He (the Word) became flesh and put that Word into action. (John 1:14)

He showed what true love is by becoming a weak human, dying a very painful death and rising from that death. He didn't do any of this for a paycheck or so people would notice His muscles. He did all this out of love for His swimmers. He did it for you and me.

Jesus jumped in, sacrificed His life and provided rescue.

Before they get in, a good lifeguard will tell the other swimmers to get to safety first or tells the other lifeguard to watch the other swimmers.

God is omnipresent, so He doesn't need a backup lifeguard or to worry about the other swimmers while He takes care of the one. He can take care of us all at the same time. (Proverbs 15:3, Psalm 139) He is willing to leave the other swimmers for the one drowning though. (Matthew 18:10-14) He is willing to jump in, go the distance it takes to get the drowning swimmer, all while being able to keep tabs on everyone in the water.

Jesus never looses track of you and loves you enough to swim to you no matter how far you have drifted.

Changes

I went through training to be a lifeguard when I was 18. After three years, I had the chance to renew my license by simply taking a test. Instead of taking the test, I chose to go through training again. I probably would have passed the renewal test, but I wanted to be a good lifeguard and be refreshed on all the information.

While I was going through training again, I found out that one or two things had been changed. For example, the amount of times you press down on the chest while doing CPR had changed. Also, I did training in a different pool and had a different instructor, so I was able to see the different styles of life-guarding. Training the second time was not necessary, but it equipped me to be a better lifeguard.

The rules have changed a little again since I was a lifeguard, but God thankfully hasn't. God thought through everything before He made the world. (Genesis 1:1, Ephesians 1:4-10) He knew the first couple of humans He made would disobey Him. He knew He would have to go through pain on a cross in order for us to have an intimate relationship with Him. He knew all this and still chose to make us.

He knew His swimmers would not follow the rules and that He would have to jump in to rescue us. Now, that is love! That is dedication! It is so much more than being willing to go through hours of training a second time to be a better lifeguard. Jesus knew He would be betrayed and ignored and mistreated, but out of love chose to lifeguard for us anyway. Even though He knew we would dirty the beautiful pool He made, He let us swim in it anyway.

His love is unconditional. No matter what we do, His love does not change and neither do His boundaries.

If you are struggling with thinking you do not deserve God's love and forgiveness, you don't. None of us flawed humans deserve Christ's faithful unwavering love. We will never be good enough to deserve it. The beautiful part is, Jesus is good enough!

It does not matter what sin you have done or how far you have drifted. It does not matter what background you have come from. What matters is if you know Jesus, because Jesus is the only One who can make things right. With His forgiveness we are cleaned from the dirty poop-stenched lake. (1 John 1:9) We do not deserve His forgiveness, but when we humbly ask Jesus for it, He will give us undeserved mercy and grace. (Proverbs 28:13)

Dive Deeper

Memory Verse:
Romans 5:8
"but God shows his love for us in that
while we were still sinners,
Christ died for us."

Now would be a great time to read John 10:7-18. When you read it, you will see Jesus being referred to as Shepherd and all the people who follow Him as His sheep.

A shepherd and lifeguard have a lot in common. Both keep watch and do what it takes to keep who they are watching safe. It talks about how the real shepherd has an investment in the sheep and actually cares for and about the sheep.

Whether you look at God as Lifeguard or Shepherd, just know how much He has invested in you and cares deeply for you. He invested because He cares. He keeps watch over us because He loves us. When you read this passage, you can replace Shepherd with Lifeguard and sheep with swimmers (if you want to!).

Matthew 18:10-14 talks about Jesus being willing to leave the ninety-nine to find the one who is lost. The Bible refers to God/Jesus as the Good Shepherd a lot. Like I said, shepherds and lifeguards have so much in common.

He gave His life for His "swimmers!" And remember, He "jumped in" even though we were not following the rules. His love is greater than any rule we break. You cannot out-sin Christ's love. In the next chapter we will go over surrendering to our Lifeguard, but for now think on this:

God doesn't change, because He is perfect. You cannot fix perfection. People sometimes try to align Jesus to fit their lifestyle, but God's boundaries/laws stay the same whether we stray from them or not. God's love stays the same no matter what we do. He is not trying to be a control-freak, He simply knows what is safe, healthy, and best and is trying to get us there.

~ 4 ~

MAY I SAVE YOU?

When a lifeguard sees a person needs help, if the person is conscious and able to give consent, they ask permission to help them. I was never given refusal, the person saw their need and excepted my help. When it is a physical problem, it is easier to see the need than if it is a spiritual issue.

We are all in spiritual need of rescuing. Jesus came to earth as a man to seek and save that which is lost. (Luke 19:10) In lifeguard talk: Jesus came to see the swimmers who are doing the dead man float and get them out, because He knows they are not just playing. We all start off dead in sin and have no hope of rescue without Jesus, because He is the only one qualified to spiritually rescue us from the filth we have gotten ourselves into.

Call For Rescue

When a lifeguard gets to a person that is conscious, they have to get permission in order to treat them. When Jesus reaches a spiritually dead person, it is up to that person whether they will receive the rescue Jesus offers.

Before someone can ask for help, they have to see their need. People don't usually go to the doctor unless they are injured or sick. When a person is drowning, they usually start flailing their arms and attempt to call for help. Calling for help is the permission a lifeguard needs.

Jesus sees we are drowning and is waiting for us to call on Him for help. The cool thing is, we do not have to wait for Him to swim to us, He has done that part already. He has already done all the work, He is just waiting for us to call on Him.

> For "everyone who calls on the name of the Lord will be
> saved."
> Romans 10:13

First Lifeguard

It can be very humbling to admit we need help. I like being the helper more than the weakling needing help. But, the truth is, I do need Jesus. I cannot live a life of purpose without Him. Actually, I cannot live life at all without Him. In Acts 3:15 Jesus is referred to as the Author of life. John 1:3 says that all things were made from God and without Him nothing would exist.

Did you know God was the first recorded lifeguard?

> "then the Lord God formed the man of dust from the ground
> and breathed into his nostrils the breath of life,
> and the man became a living creature."
> Genesis 2:7

God is perfect and sees the needs human lifeguards miss. He sees we all need Him. That is why He offers His service to us and waits for our answer.

Jesus longs to save each person from that dirty puddle they are in. That is why He went through the training and jumped in. He is qualified and is waiting on us to stop fighting against Him. If we want to truly live, we need to let Him be the guide/guard/interceder in our life.

Dive Deeper
Memory Verse:
Romans 10:13
For "everyone who calls on the name of the Lord
will be saved."

In Joel 2 it was prophesied that the Holy Spirit would be poured out on everyone who called on the Lord. If you have not done that, now would be a great time. If you have, I am so glad!

After I sign consent papers to get treated by a doctor, I have to then sit still and allow the doctor to look me over and hopefully treat me for what is wrong. If you have given God consent, I want to encourage you to sit still and let Him work on healing you. He might not heal you in the way you expect, but He is the only one who is able to look at your heart and treat your spirit.

A human doctor doesn't always know what the problem is and cannot always treat it, but God knows what the problem is and knows how to heal you.

What this looks like spiritually: Admit to God that you have messed up and ask Him to forgive you. Start obeying what He has asked you to do. He knows you will mess up here and there, but His rescue does not depend on your perfection. His rescue was started by Him knowing your need and loving you. When you give Him consent and lean on Him, like you're going to learn about in a couple of chapters, He will intercede for you and watch over you.

In future chapters we will learn how to lean on Him and trust Him, but for now I want you to read Psalm 46 and then practice what He says to do in verse 10; be still and know that He is God.

~ 5 ~

GO BEHIND

When I was in lifeguard training, we had to learn how to rescue a person from drowning. In order for a lifeguard to protect him/herself while rescuing a person who was drowning they must go behind the person. Then they get the buoy under the person's back and get a good hold on the person, usually like a choke-hold around each shoulder.

We go behind, because the person who is flailing their arms can panic and grab for the lifeguard. This can cause the lifeguard and the person in trouble to both drown. I was able to get a better grip on the person from the back and if they are leaning back, their legs don't get in the way of my swimming.

When doing lifeguard training, we took turns saving someone and acting like the person needing to be saved. When I was the person being saved, I did not always see my lifeguard friend coming. I had to trust they were going to have my back. I believed they would be there even though I did not see them and trusted that they would get to me in the time I needed them to.

Seeing as I am still alive, they made it in time every time! I did have my doubts here and there, but I did not allow my feelings to control my actions. I waited, even though it was not always easy and my friend always got me out.

Feeling Vs Fact

We do not always see what God is doing. Sometimes when we don't see Him working, we might feel like He doesn't care, like some big, callous jerk. Feelings and facts are two different things. The truth is, God cares deeper than any ocean and is always there. (Proverbs 15:3, 1 Peter 5:7) He is there and He has our back. He has calloused hands, but a very soft heart for His swimmers.

There have been moments where I questioned if God was real and, if He was, why He allowed me to go through certain trials and struggles. There were times I felt extremely alone and unwanted. I felt ugly and hopeless. The truth is, on my own there was no hope. Without my cleansing Redeemer all I had were filthy clothes from the muck I was swimming in. (Isaiah 64:6)

But God, in His perfect love, went the distance for me. He worked in ways I could not see. Things that I truly believed would be my undoing turned into things that helped me see my need for The Rescuer.

These evil things that had been done to me and that I chose to do are not things of which God approved. Somehow, He was able to shine bright in my darkest hours and turn my sad heart into a joyful heart. You see, He showed me so gently that I could trust Him. He showed me by His actions that I was loved and that He treasured me. He has been renewing my mind and turning my thoughts to what is truly beautiful. What I thought was ugly and hopeless, God is turning into radiant light.

Darkness

It's hard to see anything while in the dark. Not trying to offend, but that is how the Bible describes people who are living without Jesus Christ. (John 8:12) God is described as light and in Him there is no darkness. (1 John 1:5) First John 2 says there is no need to stumble when you have light. We might not see everything God is doing and we might have our doubts, but know that He is there and will not let anyone spiritually drown when they repent and call on Him. (John 6:37)

John 11:10
"But if anyone walks in the night, he stumbles,
because the light is not in him."

Daniel 2:21-22 says,
"He changes times and seasons;
he removes kings and sets up kings;
he gives wisdom to the wise
and knowledge to those who have understanding;
he reveals deep and hidden things;
he knows what is in the darkness,
and the light dwells with him."

Dive Deeper

If you would read Mark 4:35-41, you would find Jesus and his students in a boat during a really bad storm. Jesus seems to be asleep and the students who had seen Jesus do several miracles asked Him if He cared about what happens to them. During a storm is when you usually see who a person truly is. You can see doubt, fear, anger, and sometimes faith. Who are you when times get rough?

Who do you want to be?

Just like Jesus went the distance to give you life, He can help get you spiritually where you want to be. All you have to do is ask and follow Him.

Sometimes it might feel like God's not paying attention or like He doesn't care. No matter how we feel, He is watching and He does care. He wants us to have faith. He sometimes goes places on our behalf we cannot see and we do not even know about. He sometimes waits to grab us, so we can see where our faith truly is. Are you going to trust Him to have your back?

If you have called to Him and have submitted to the Lifeguard, that means He is your friend. If He is your Lifeguard friend, have patience. When you cannot see Him it does not mean He is not going to rescue you. Remember, He has already swum the distance and is there, just wait on His timing, because He may just want to show you something with that storm.

Some types of "storms" in life He does not approve of, but will figure out a way to work it all together for your good as you trust Him and allow Him to do the work.

Hebrews 11 is what some call the faith chapter. It says that faith is assurance of things hoped for and the conviction of things not seen. I love in verse 4 when it says that even though he died, the faith of Abel still speaks. In verse 5 it said that Enoch was commended by God for his faith. Then it says without faith we cannot please God.

In order to please God we must believe He exists and that we will eventually be rewarded for seeking Him. Having reverent fear like Noah, painful obedience like Abraham, bravery like Moses and his parents, and hospitality like Rahab is what we should strive for. It is such an inspiring chapter to me and if you have not read it yet, you should.

Memory Verse:
2 Corinthians 4:18 (NIV)
"So we fix our eyes not on what is seen,
but on what is unseen,
since what is seen is temporary,
but what is unseen is eternal."

If you read verses 16-18 in 2 Corinthians 4 it will make more sense. The things we see may seem scary. Sometimes it may feel like the issues we have are too great and will never end. Take heart my friends, God has the back of anyone who calls on Him and, though we don't always see the results right away, the things we do for the Lord will last forever.

~ 6 ~

TRUST ME

In the next two chapters I will be talking about leaning on the lifeguard and not tensing up. It is much easier for me to do those two things when I trust the person and their ability.

So, I told you about Jesus loving us enough to go through training and jumping in. I told you about Him waiting for you to call to Him so He can save you from your dilemma. I truly hope you have called out to the Lord for Him to save you. If you haven't, what are you waiting for? I am praying that by the end of this book you will call to Him, trust Him enough to lean on Him without tensing up, follow His leading, and point others to Him.

This chapter is about trusting The Almighty Lifeguard. It ties in quite a bit with the last chapter. When I cannot see Him, I know He is there. When I am in a rough storm, I can look back and remember the previous things God has brought me through. He is trustworthy and wants to walk you through the storms of life.

Taste Goodness

I spoke in the last chapter about not always being able to see the person saving me. I then spoke a little about how it can be hard waiting for it to happen. I find myself putting my trust in things that do not make sense sometimes. There are things that go beyond common sense that God can use to showcase how amazing

He is, but there are some things that I sometimes trust even when I know it will eventually not be good for me.

I know that if I start my morning with bleached flour I will not have as much pep-and-go as I would with a spinach-filled smoothie. When my family first started drinking smoothies, the only thing my kids could see was spinach. They heard me say it would help them feel good, but they didn't understand that I could also make that smoothie taste delicious. Not all my children want to drink them, but the ones that do almost always want more. Not to toot my own horn, but I do make some amazing smoothies! It does not always look better than what is at the bakery, but in the afternoon I never regret my healthy decision.

Some of you are probably wondering why I would bring up smoothies and pastries. When my kids knew I had their best interest in mind and I had made delicious foods in the past, it made it easier for them to trust me with their taste buds. Just like I want my children to be healthy in every way, our heavenly Father is wanting the same for us.

My kids love candy and all the junk food the people around them eat. I know that some of it is not as addictive as others. I know that some is not as unhealthy. But it is all called junk food for a reason! I love my kids and I don't want them to treat themselves like trash cans. As I write this I am convicted at how much junk I have allowed my children to consume.

One big difference between me and God is I usually feed my kids good things, but good is all God offers. We are the ones who sometimes opt out and go the unhealthy route. Physically and spiritually. We might not always like what God offers us, but He will never give us "junk". Other people might give us junk and we blame Him for not intercepting it. He might give us food for our spiritual health and we see it as junk.

Taste Buds

Did you know that our taste buds change every three months? Too bad our habits usually stay the same. When we eat right our taste buds usually start craving good things. Psalm 34:8-10 tells us to taste and see that the Lord is good! Do not use your body or mind as a trash can any longer. God is so good and is so good for you!

If you are used to spiritual bleached flour and switch to spiritual smoothies, it might take a while to adjust. You might still have cravings from time to time, but I want to encourage you to stay on track, because in the afternoon you will not regret your healthy choice.

I know smoothies and Jesus are two totally different things. Jesus is offering much more than a blender full of goodness. He is offering to give you living water. He is offering to make you into a cup overflowing and help you never run dry. (John 4:10-14) (Isaiah 58:11)

He never said you would always crave Him or have a flawless life. He is not a politician, He will never lie to you or make you empty promises so you will vote for Him. He does make promises, but He has and will keep every promise He has made.

I can trust Him because He has kept all His promises in the past and I believe He will keep the ones yet to come.

God's Faithfulness

The Israelite people had been slaves in Egypt for years (Which God told Abraham would happen in Genesis 15:13-14). God heard their cries for help and got them out of slavery. They were thirsty, God provided water. They were hungry, God provided food. When they didn't like the meatless options, God provided meat. While the leader God gave the people was getting directions from God, the people got tired of waiting and made themselves a god they could see. (Exodus1-32)

They were not patient enough to wait for their Lifeguard. They had been cared for and given freedom from slavery, but they did not all trust the One who got them to freedom. It can be very hard to wait sometimes. It can sometimes feel very vulnerable. God knows that and wants you to trust Him anyway. Remember, He is the Lifeguard of your soul, not your every whim. He is working on renewing your mind and refining your heart. He knows that sometimes in order to do that, He needs to wait a little while before He reveals things to you.

Isaiah 41:10
"fear not, for I am with you;
be not dismayed, for I am your God;
I will strengthen you,
I will help you,
I will uphold you with my righteous right hand."

His ways are not our ways, and that is a good thing. (Isaiah 55:8-9) He is not just thinking about our earthly bodies, He is preparing us for eternity. He cares very much what happens to us.

Proverbs 19:23 says that reverence of the Lord leads to life. A healthy fear of The Lifeguard is the start of getting us to safety. Please notice that I said a healthy fear. God does not want us to tremble every time He talks to us. He wants us to have the right respect for Him and know He is in authority. We are to be quick to listen to our Lifeguard and quick to obey for our own good.

Dive Deeper

Memory Verse:
Isaiah 12:2
"Behold, God is my salvation;
I will trust, and will not be afraid;
for the Lord God is my strength and my song,
and he has become my salvation."

Have you ever blamed God for things that have gone wrong?

Is there anything holding you back from trusting Him completely?

If you read John 4:7-15 you will see Jesus using water as a picture of what He offers. If you could put what Christ offers in one sentence, what would it be?

Without Him we will always live with a void and He is offering to help us never lack anything good. Read Psalm 34 and see what jumps out at you.

~ 7 ~

LEAN ON ME

In this stage of the rescue the lifeguard has jumped in, swum to you, gotten your permission, and has gone behind you. The lifeguard would then hold each of your arms and get your back onto the buoy. They would get you to lean back and relax. We will go over relaxing later, but for now let's concentrate on leaning back.

When the swimmer is leaning on the tube, it makes it easier to hold them up and places some of their weight on the tube. When the person is leaning, it makes it easier to swim with them, which makes saving them much easier. It would be easier to wait for a swimmer to go unconscious than try to swim with them if they are still flailing. They must stop flailing and trust the lifeguard enough to surrender their fighting. A person drowning must surrender to their lifeguard in order to be rescued.

Trust Fall

So now that you have a picture of a swimmer leaning on their lifeguard, I want you to picture Jesus as that lifeguard. Are you leaning on Him? It's one thing to know someone needs help, it's another thing to help them. It's one thing to say you trust someone, but are you actually putting your trust in Jesus?

Here's another way to look at it. Have you ever seen or participated in a "trust fall?" A person stands with their back towards someone and falls toward them. The person can say they will fall back, but until they actually do it, it's not a trust fall.

In James 2 a man named Paul was explaining faith to someone. He said that he would show them his faith through his works. This is a great chapter, you should totally read it! If Paul was speaking lifeguard, he would say something like: "All the training a lifeguard does, doesn't really matter if all he does afterwards is sit on the side of the pool. Jesus got in the water for us. We now are able to lean on Him. But it doesn't count as a rescue if we do not lean on and follow the Rescuer."

Signed Copy

A sweet friend of mine told me that she wanted me to sign her copy of The Care Giver. So, I waited for her to bring it to me. A couple months went by and no sign of the book. She found out I had signed someone else's copy. She reminded me that she had been waiting for me to sign hers. I then told her, she had to bring it to me and then I would willingly sign it.

It's pretty much the same with us and God. We need to not only ask for His help. We need to surrender our plans and way of life in order to get a fail-proof plan and a life overflowing with purpose.

I did not ask my friend to give me her book so I could mess it up. I wanted to bless her by personalizing her book. Jesus is not trying to mess anything up for us. He is trying to redeem us and give us a personalized relationship with God.

Lay It Down

If any person swims long enough, they will eventually get tired. There will be times people get cramps or run out of energy and feel they cannot go any further.

In life, we get tired and discouraged. There have been times in my life when I had no idea how I was going to make it through another day. If that is you, I have the answer! If that is not you, eventually it will be, so you can read this and put it away for later.

Here are a few things the Bible says about this:

"Are you tired? Worn out? Burned out on religion?
Come to me. Get away with me and you'll recover your life.
I'll show you how to take a real rest.
Walk with me and work with me - watch how I do it.
Learn the unforced rhythms of grace.
I won't lay anything heavy or ill-fitting on you.
Keep company with me and you'll learn to live freely and
lightly."
Matthew 11:28-30 (MSG)

"Humble yourselves, therefore, under the mighty hand of God
so that at the proper time he may exalt you,
casting all your anxieties on him,
because he cares for you."
1 Peter 5:6-7

"Trust in the Lord with all your heart,
and lean not on your own understanding.
In all your ways acknowledge him,
and he shall direct your paths."
Proverbs 3:5-6 (NKJV)

When the Bible talks about putting your trust and hope in God, it means actually surrendering everything to Him and lean back. Trust Him enough to put your faith in Him. It's not a "trust fall" without the fall.

Dive Deeper

Memory Verse:
Proverbs 3:5
"Trust in the Lord with all your heart,
and do not lean on your own understanding."

When I tell you that we are to lean on Jesus, this does not always mean a reclining position. Sometimes it means to take a step in faith like Peter did. One day Peter and his student buddies were in a boat and there was a storm. This time, Jesus was not physically in the boat with them and they saw something on the water. They heard Jesus' voice saying it was Him. Peter said back, "If that is really you, tell me to come to you on the water."

This event happened in Matthew 14:22-33. If you were to read it, you would see that Peter took at least a couple steps out of the boat. It was only when he stopped focusing on Jesus and saw the strong storm around him that he began to sink. Jesus was a Good Lifeguard and helped Peter up when he called for help.

It does not matter how many times you sink, Jesus will help you every time you call to Him. Leaning on Him does not mean expecting Him to do what you want Him to while you relax on a cruise. Leaning on Him is trusting His plan more than your plan. It is about trusting His understanding and trust Him enough to obey.

Have you asked Him to forgive you of the things you have done wrong?

Keeping in mind that it is not a "trust fall" without the fall, have you truly leaned on Jesus?

Trust without the fall is not true faith. Without faith it is impossible to please God. It's time to hand over our "books" to Him and let Him write on them what He wants. He wants to make things personal (in a complete and pure way). You have to let Him know where you want the relationship to be and allow Him to get you there.

~ 8 ~

TENSE

At this point, the swimmer is leaning back on the lifeguard and the tube that is between them. It is much easier to swim with a person, pretty much on top of you, if they are relaxed.

When I was in training I struggled to get one of my co-lifeguards out of the water. He was pretending he was unconscious. He was so heavy! He had a lot of muscle and that had something to do with it, but another thing that made him seem heavier was how tense he was. When you get tense and tighten your muscles, it makes you heavier in the water. This is embarrassing to admit, but it took me close to three minutes to get my friend out of the water. I did much better the next time!

One reason my lifeguard pal was so tense, was because we had just started training and it was my first time getting someone out of the water. (And remember, I had just learned how to swim!) After I built up my muscles and practiced, I was much quicker and had more confidence. When a person has been life-guarding a while, there is no need for the swimmer to tense up. When they do, it makes it harder on the person trying to rescue them and does nothing for the swimmer.

Focus and Trust

If you have called to Jesus for rescue from sin and are leaning on Him, relax! There is nothing too heavy for Him, so He'll be able to rescue you even if you are a little tense. But, I promise you, there is no reason to be.

I sometimes get tense when I come across waves in my life that threaten me. I sometimes get distracted by debris in the water. Even Peter, one of the men following Jesus in ministry, got distracted. Jesus was actually walking on the water and gave Peter the ability to walk on the water too!

Peter started looking at the storm around him and got scared and began to sink. When Jesus helped Peter up, Jesus said, "O you of little faith, why did you doubt?" (Matthew 14:22-33)

I love how gentle Jesus was with Peter. He could have given Peter a speech about how stupid he was for not trusting Jesus after all he had seen, but didn't. Jesus lovingly assured Peter that there was no reason to doubt.

When we are in the middle of life's storms, we can walk with our hearts toward Jesus, knowing He can take care of any storm we go through. If you read the Matthew 14 passage I spoke about, you would discover that Jesus helped Peter in the boat and then calmed the wind.

There are two times in the book of Mark that Jesus is recorded calming a storm. Before He calmed the first one in chapter 4, the men He was with got anxious and asked Jesus if He even cared. I know I already wrote a little about this, but sometimes we need reminding that during storms is when our faith it tested.

I hate taking tests! I can sometimes be a perfectionist, I want everything I do to be perfect. I want to get a perfect score or not take the test at all. As I live and grow, I know that there is only one thing in my life that has to be perfect: the Friend I am in the storm with. Peter started to sink when he saw the waves around him. When he remembered it was not HIM, but THEM, that is when he put his focus back where it belonged.

You and I are not alone. It might feel like we are at times, but feelings and facts are two very different things.

Dive Deeper

Memory Verse:
"Do not be anxious about anything,
but in everything
by prayer and supplication
with thanksgiving
let your requests be made known to God.
And the peace of God, which surpasses all understanding,
will guard your hearts and your minds in Christ Jesus."
Philippians 4:6-7

Let's go ahead and read Matthew 6:19-34. Don't worry like the people without a lifeguard, your Lifeguard can see what all is happening. He has provided in the past and will continue to provide as we store our treasures in heaven. We decide where we put our trust and where we lean. We also decide what we are going to focus most of our attention on.

We cannot always control the random impure thoughts that pop in our minds, but we can decide whether we are going to dwell on them or not. The Bible tells us in Philippians 4:8-9 about what we are to think. What do you think would help your thoughts stay on what is true, honorable, just, pure and lovely?

One thing that has really been helping me think on wonderful things is being intentional about what I watch, read and listen to. I used to try to avoid "polluted" things. Along the way I realized me just trying to avoid things made me notice them more and think on them more. I had to intentionally choose what I was going to focus on and actually focus on that thing.

It's like dieting: when I try to avoid certain foods, those foods are what I want the most. It only works if I know what I need to eat and concentrate on what my body needs.

I grew up with attention problems. I have always had a hard time concentrating with things going on around me or when things are a certain way. In high school and college I started figuring out things that would help me study and what my main triggers were.

I could totally make excuses for my "squirrel" mentality or I could figure out what is a priority and with God's help focus on what matters. I want to focus on what lies on the other side of the storm, because focusing on the storm gets me nowhere. What do you want to focus on?

Philippians 4:8 tells you what you should focus your thoughts on. Verse 9 tells us that as we practice these things the God of peace will be with us.

What is something you get from 1 Peter 3:8-12?

Please read Psalm 139:1-18. Soak up the fact that our caring Creator is always with you, can always see you and will always hear you. He is both humble and mighty. He is strong enough to get you to the right kind of water and loving enough to care about what happens to you.

Do not be anxious about your life, you have the best lifeguard! No one could do better.

"I have said these things to you,
that in me you may have peace.
In the world you will have tribulation.
But take heart;

I have overcome the world."
John 16:33

~ 9 ~

FOLLOW GUIDE

The lifeguard has now jumped in, swam to the person, and has gotten the person to lean back on them. Now what? Well, if the person is unconscious, the lifeguard simply gets them to shore as quickly as possible. I am not going to go into all the details about things like if the person hit their head or may have a spinal injury. In this chapter we are going to cover what the lifeguard does when the person is awake.

The truth is, we all started off spiritually dead. When we called out for Jesus to save us, He did and gave us true life. So at this point we, as the swimmer, are awake and fully trusting in the Ultimate Lifeguard. What now?

Now, if the swimmer is able and there is a long distance to cover, the lifeguard gets the swimmer to kick their feet in the direction the lifeguard tells them to.

Start Kicking

So, what would spiritual kicking look like? It is pretty much following the Lifeguard's instructions. When you feel like you should give food to someone or tell someone about Jesus, that is the Holy Spirit telling you to "kick." Later in this book we will look at telling others about our rescue and the Lifeguard who saved us, but for now we are going to concentrate on obeying and understanding God's directions.

We do not have to understand the whys, we just need to do what God asks us to do. He is the best Lifeguard, He knows where the shore is, and He knows how to get us there. Following His directions is the wisest thing we could ever do.

Once we get spiritually awakened and are trusting Jesus, we need to do what He says. We have been rescued at a very high price and need to heed the warnings our Lifeguard gives us. God gives amazing advise through His Word, the Bible. Not every thought and feeling we get is from the Lord, after all we do still live in the flesh. When you get an idea that you need to do something, first thing you should do is see if it aligns with the manual God gave us.

"Hear instruction and be wise, and do not neglect it."
Blessed is the one who listens to me (wisdom),
watching daily at my gates, waiting beside my doors."
Proverbs 8:33-34

We should stay close to the Lifeguard so we can hear His instructions. If you are wondering how you can stay close to God, keep reading!

Stay Close

One way I can be close to someone is by listening to them and getting to know them. We can get to know God by reading the Bible and asking Him to reveal Himself to us (2 Timothy 4:6-17). If we seek to know Him, He will make Himself known to us.

God has already told us which direction to kick. He has told us that the greatest thing is to love God with all we have and love others like we would ourselves. (Matthew 22:35-40) The other commands pretty much show us how to love God and others.

How to love

I guess 1 Corinthians 13:4-7 would be the most likely place to start when we talk about love, because it is referred to as the love chapter. If we are to show others love we are to be patient with them and kind to them. We should find ways to enrich people's lives instead of wanting what they have. Acting in love means we should be polite and not act like we are better than the people around us. We should forgive easily and look out for the well being of others.

Micah 6:8 is so clear that God has already told us what He wants from us. He wants us to do justice, love kindness, and walk humbly with Him.

We know we are to love God and others, that is very clear throughout scripture. There will be times when you might be faced with a moral dilemma. When this happens, Jesus said that the Holy Spirit would guide us into truth. The Holy Spirit convicts us of the wrong we do and helps us see what is righteous. (John 16:8-15)

Even when I walk (or swim) in the roughest storm I do not need to be afraid of anything if God is with me. His guidance and un-changing boundaries comfort me and help me feel safe and confi-dent. (Psalm 23:4)

Dive Deeper

Memory Verse:
Psalm 73:24
"You guide me with your counsel,
and afterward you will receive me to glory."

In the next chapter we will talk about God receiving us to glory. For now, let's concentrate on being led by His counsel.

If you take the time to read 2 Timothy 3:16-17 you will see that the scripture is from God. The Bible is a great source for teaching and correcting and training people to be righteous. The Bible is our training manual. God gave us the instructions needed to live a righteous life. As we follow the Spirit's leading and read the manual, we will be able to walk through any storm. As we gain the right perspective those storms are no longer going to have the same effect on us. The Bible instructs and the Spirit equips.

Yes, we will still get wet. Yes, we will still face struggles. But, in the midst of those waves and debris stands our Solid Rock! (Matthew 7:24-25)

Please read Philippians 2:3-16. We are to allow the love of Christ to shine through us in this dark world. Simply by not complaining, a woman I knew when I was a teenager showed me what Jesus looked like. I want to encourage you to "hold fast to the word of life" and be obedient to God even when things don't make sense. Are you showing others what Jesus looks like with your way of life?

If not, there's no greater time than the present! All we have to do to show Christ to others is follow Him and allow Him to teach us.

THE ULTIMATE LIFEGUARD ~ 55

Now read John 14:15-27. We cannot show love with disobedience. Do you love Jesus?

If you believe God is directing you to go somewhere or do something, follow His lead. He knows where you are and where the shore is and how to get you to that shore. For now, trust and obey through the calm and storms of life. If you are leaning on Him, He has your back and will not leave you in the water alone.

~ 10 ~

MAIN GOAL

In this chapter we are going to go over why the lifeguard has gone through all this work. What is the end goal? My goal as a lifeguard is to get the drowning person to a place where they are safe and healthy. I am looking out for their well being. I want the swimmers under my watch to enjoy themselves, but not at the expense of their safety.

Our Ultimate Lifeguard is wanting us to have joy while we "swim" through life, but He knows the end goal is more important than our temporary comfort or entertainment.

Just like I want all my swimmers to be able to swim well, Christ wants us to know how to live well. Just like I am working to get my swimmers to a healthy and safe place, God is working to bring us to a permanent home that has no waves or debris. Until we get to our final destination, we should study the manual our Lifeguard has given us (I'm talking about the Bible) and follow the Holy Spirit's leading.

On The Shore

Because of what Jesus did on the cross and in the tomb, you and I have a chance to live a life of purpose and die with assurance of our final destination. (Ephesians 1:13-24) When we say yes to the rescue Jesus offers, we can live a life unafraid and unashamed.

When we ask Jesus to save us from sin, we should swim the way He tells us to.

We are not supposed to do what the Israelites did. After God set them free from slavery, when they were faced with tough situations, they wanted to go back to the place they were enslaved. (Numbers 14:4) When we are set free from the grip sin has on us and the consequences of that sin, we need to submit to God and resist the devil. (James 4:7)

No more trying to hold onto things that chained us in the past. If you have called to Jesus, confessed Him with your mouth and believed in Him with your heart, that means He has taken the chains of sin off of you. Now that the chains are off and the door of the prison is open, we need to get out of the cell.

We no longer have to stumble around like we did when we had no light. We have been set free and we are to live like we are free!

1 Peter 2:24-25
"He himself bore our sins in His body on the tree,
that we might die to sin and live to righteousness.
By his wounds you have been healed.
For you were straying like sheep,
but have now returned to the Shepherd and Overseer of your souls."

Paul, in 1 Timothy 1, was warning his dear friend about false teachings. In verse 5 he told how he was writing out of love with a pure heart, clear conscience, and sincere faith. Those three things are what Jesus is aiming to give us.

I apologize in advance if this next part seems rough. I do not like a lot of fluff, which is why my books are on the shorter side. I appreciate when people are honest and direct with me, so that is what I will try to be with you.

... Ever After

Honestly, this chapter has been the hardest for me to write. It is easy to write about things I have experienced, but I have not seen the shore yet. I have read about it, but the Bible tells me I can't even image what it will be like (1 Corinthians 2:9). When Jesus was talking to His disciples He told them that He was going to prepare a place for them (John 14:3).

While doing research for this chapter, one thing I found interesting is that God did not prepare hell for unbelievers like I had thought. He prepared hell for Satan and his demons (Matthew 25:41). Heaven is intended for the people He made and loves. Hell is intended for all the fallen angels. Yes, people who do not believe in Jesus as Christ will go with those angels, but I hope and pray you will not be among them.

This chapter tells you how important the next chapter is. The next chapter is about telling other swimmers about your rescue and how they can be rescued. This chapter tells us why this is so important.

I have been guilty in the past of not sharing the good news of Jesus when the opportunity was available. In the past, I unintentionally cared more about people not rejecting me than helping them see what their situation was. Today, I want everyone to know Jesus, I just don't always know what to say to make that happen. Sometimes not knowing the right words to say makes me not want to say any.

Here's the situation: Everyone who does not have Jesus as their Lifeguard will spend eternity without Him. I do not like to think about this, because I like my stories to have happy endings. I do not like the fact that hell exists and most people are going to spend eternity there. So I have a choice, I can either ignore the unhappy ever afters or I can do what I can to point people to the Lifeguard and pray they accept His help.

I used to paint God as the bad guy in my mind. But, the truth is, He has given us all a choice to be brought to the beautiful place He is preparing for us or do things on our own and face judgment alone (John 5:28-29, Acts 17:30-31). He loves us and wants us all to know Him and be rescued, but He also is a just God and will in the end give the consequences to the choices we make. He is a good parent, He doesn't give idle threats.

Dive Deeper

Memory Verse:
Colossians 3:23-24 (NLT)
"Work willingly at whatever you do,
as though you were working for the Lord
rather than for people.
Remember that the Lord will give you
an inheritance as your reward,
and that the Master you are serving is Christ."

In Psalm 25 there were many things that popped out at me while working on this study. What stands out to you?

I want us to look at 1 Corinthians 10:1-21 and verse 31. Most of the time when I read this, I concentrate on the verse about God not letting me be tempted past my capacity. This time it was how we are not to be like the people who had been set free and yet did not live in freedom. They lived in a slavery mentality and did not honor the One who set them free. In this scripture we are told to look at them as an example. I want you to read the passage and look at what stands out to you. What can we learn from these people?

Are you living a free-from-sin life? Or, are you holding onto your chains?

Give those things over to the Lord and allow Him to carry you to shore. Better yet, let's walk or run through life with Jesus as our focus. This world is not worth an eternity without Jesus.

Please read 1 Peter 1:3-9 and 1:13-25. Then read Matthew 13:47-50.

I am not trying to scare you, but at the same time, I want you to know where your choice will get you in the long run. What do you choose and who are you bringing with you?

~ 11 ~

OTHER SWIMMERS

Sometimes people will go against the pool rules because they want other swimmers to like them. Some swimmers don't understand the pool rules that are on the sign. Maybe someone put their towel on the sign and they didn't even know the rules were there. No matter the reason, there are rules that everyone should follow, but eventually someone messes up.

I wonder if you know where I'm going with this. Everyone on this planet has gone against God's law at one point or another, whether they meant to or not. None of us is perfect, which is why we needed Jesus to save us.

Like the beautiful picture Jesus and Peter gave us in the Gospels, we are to focus on Jesus to keep from sinking. We need to follow God's commands while in the waters of life. We need to encourage others to do the same and point them to the life-giving Guard of our souls.

This is where being fishers of men comes in. Jesus told some of His disciples that if they would follow Him, He would make them fishers of men. (Matthew 4:19) We are to encourage others to rise above the dangerous waters and walk toward Jesus. We are still in the world, but should not have worldly values. (John 17:11-26) When the people who are asleep see how we swim or walk and hear what Jesus has done in our lives it can inspire them to turn to our Lifeguard. (Matthew 5:14-16)

Don't Go Back

Now that you are rescued, I want to encourage you to not get back into the same spiritual waters Jesus saved you from. There will be other swimmers that will not understand why you "swim" differently. Some will probably get angry at your change. Some people might belittle who Christ is and what He has done for you. And there may be moments when that bleached cinnamon roll looks too tempting to pass up. When those moments come, remember what swimming the old way was truly like and where it was leading you. Remember, those moments will pass, but Christ and His stability last forever.

Like the priest in Acts 5, there will be people who are jealous of your freedom and the light God equips you to shine with. I am inspired by Peter and his friends in verses 29-32 when they pretty much said God's instructions were the ones they would follow. They were going to tell others about their Rescuer no matter what other swimmers did to them, because they valued the instructions of their Lifeguard more than the popularity of other swimmers. They cared more about the people they were sharing with than others' opinions of them.

It makes no sense to follow mortal, spiritually dead swimmers when there is an immortal Lifeguard giving clear, life-giving directions. The Lifeguard can see all and is wanting what is best for His swimmers. Other swimmers are very limited in what they can see and are usually looking out for themselves before looking out for you. I would rather put my hope and trust in a Lifeguard offering me a better view and destination than swimmers who just want me to stay in meaningless and unsatisfying waters.

Solid Rock

Whether the foundation you have under your feet is sand or rock, there will still be storms. You will still struggle. You will experience pain and disappointments in life. The difference in the end, is one stands strong and the other crumbles. (Matthew 7:24-27)

As Jesus guards our hearts and provides a strong foundation, we are to be guards as well. We are to be on guard and stand firm in our faith and we are to do everything out of love. (1 Corinthians 16:13-14) It will not always be easy to stand your ground, but remember this: You are not standing alone!

Dive Deeper

Jesus' last words before going to heaven were telling us to help wake people up and point them to Jesus. He made a point of telling us that we are not alone. As we tell others of the work God is doing in our life, we can do it with confidence because He will not make us do it on our own. Yes, we may feel alone at times, but remember that feelings and facts are two different things.

Memory Verse
Matthew 28:19-20
"Go therefore and make disciples of all nations,
baptizing them in the name of the Father and of the Son and of the Holy Spirit,
teaching them to observe all that I have commanded you.
And behold,
I am with you always,
to the end of the age."

Please read Psalm 1 and Proverbs 1. We should follow the Lifeguard's instruction instead of ignorant swimmers.

Do you remember Solomon? He was King David's son and later became king. God directly gave wisdom to King Solomon and he is responsible for a majority of the book of Proverbs.

These are a few verses that stood out to me in Proverbs 1: 7,10, 22-33. Fools despise instructions. Don't give in to the foolish advise and the enticement of the people around you. Stand firm and encourage the people around you to do the same. If they listen, that's great! If they don't, don't give up! You are not alone and you have a very meaningful purpose.

Ephesians 4:29-32 tells us to be kind and encouraging to other swimmers. Help each other. You never know what storm they are going through. Also, when you reflect the love of Jesus, other swimmers will be more likely to want to hear about Jesus and your rescue.

Ezekiel 3:16-21 says to warn others of the danger ahead. Not everyone will like what you have to say. I'm sure not everyone will like what I had to say in this book. Most people might reject our message, but there may be some that listen. It could be years later when what you say to them about Jesus makes sense to them.

I want to leave you with one final thought. If you knew of a condemned building that was going to be demolished and knew there were people still inside, would you warn them?

Every body on earth is going to come to an earthly end sooner or later. The people who know Jesus have a great future ahead of them, but the people who don't are in a house that's condemned. (John 3:18) Are you going to warn them?

If you are wanting to study the Bible more and wondering where you should go from here, the book of First John would be a great place to start.

MEMORY VERSES

1. Training – God is qualified to be your Guard.

"And the peace of God, which surpasses all understanding,
will guard your hearts and your minds in Christ Jesus."
Philippians 4:7

2. Danger! - He sees what is happening and what's about to happen.

James 1:22
"But be doers of the word,
and not hearers only,
deceiving yourselves."

3. Jump In – You are His main concern.

Romans 5:8
"but God shows his love for us in that
while we were still sinners,
Christ died for us."

4. May I Save You? - Admit you need help and submit to The Rescuer.

Romans 10:13
For "everyone who calls on the name of the Lord
will be saved."

5. Go Behind – We don't always see Him working on our behalf.

2 Corinthians 4:18 (NIV)
"So we fix our eyes not on what is seen,
but on what is unseen,
since what is seen is temporary,
but what is unseen is eternal."

6. Trust Me! - Believe in the Lifeguard's ability and accept His help.

Isaiah 12:2
"Behold, God is my salvation;
I will trust, and will not be afraid;
for the Lord God is my strength and my song,
and he has become my salvation."

7. Lean On Me – Have faith enough to lean on Him.

Proverbs 3:5
"Trust in the Lord with all your heart,
and do not lean on your own understanding."

8. Tense – Letting go of tension makes rescue easier.

"Do not be anxious about anything,
but in everything by prayer and supplication
with thanksgiving
let your requests be made known to God.
And the peace of God, which surpasses all understanding,
will guard your hearts and your minds in Christ Jesus."
Philippians 4:6-7

9. Follow Guide – Follow His lead.

Psalm 73:24
"You guide me with your counsel,
and afterward you will receive me to glory."

10. Main Goal – He'll show you how to swim and bring you to shore.

Colossians 3:23-24 (NLT)
"Work willingly at whatever you do,
as though you were working for the Lord
rather than for people.
Remember that the Lord will give you
an inheritance as your reward,
and that the Master you are serving is Christ."

11. Other Swimmers – Listen to the Lifeguard while telling other swimmers about the Lifeguard who saved you.

Matthew 28:19-20
"Go therefore and make disciples of all nations,
baptizing them in the name of the Father and the Son and of the Holy Spirit,
teaching them to observe all that I have commanded you.
And behold,
I am with you always,
to the end of the age."

Note From Author

Thank you for the time you spent with me in this book. I hope it blessed you and enriched your faith as much as it has mine. I have spent several hours praying for each person who will read this book to know Jesus, trust Him, and follow His lead.

I would like to thank my sister-in-Christ, Aileen Foley for proofing and praying with me over this book.

I also want to thank my brother, Blake Chambers for doing the cover. He is a tattoo artist in Austin and is the most gifted artist I've ever seen.

A big thank you should also go to my sister-in-Christ, Stephanie Figueroa who said something one day about feeling like she was caught in a spiritual currant. That is what caused me to start seeing Jesus as our spiritual Lifeguard. Stephanie has been such an inspiration to me by how much she has been leaning on Jesus during her recent storm and being so refreshingly honest about where she is with the Lord. She has cancer and has been going through treatment, so please keep her in your prayers.

I have learned and grown so much spiritually through this study! I have been brought to tears several times with the different things God has shown me (both sorrowful tears and overwhelmed-by-God's-goodness tears). I want to make this perfectly clear, I am not an expert because I wrote a couple books. God orchestrated many things in my life and I truly believe the books I have written and are prepping to write have been given to me by God. He is the Author of life and has given me the inspiration and opportunity to be an author. Thank you, Lord for allowing me to be a part of some people's journey with you. I am honored that you would use me in this way.

No matter how big or small it may seem, God can produce life through the seeds we obediently plant. God has great plans for you, greater than any plan you could make for yourself. It is only when you follow His plans that you can make a truly lasting impact in this world.

At this point in time, I feel like God is wanting me to do a book called The Church Goer and then one called The People Pleaser. I would greatly appreciate your prayers for me to understand God's leading and for me to always follow His lead.

Until my next book, I would like to invite you to visit my blog:
puppetlady.blogspot.com

Well Guarded,
AmyAnn

www.ingramcontent.com/pod-product-compliance
Lightning Source LLC
Chambersburg PA
CBHW070448130626
46553CB00006B/2303